in · som · ni · a

Paperback: 978-1-7374675-3-3
Distributed paperback: 978-1-7374675-0-2
Audiobook: 978-1-7374675-2-6
Ebook: 978-1-7374675-1-9
Kindle: 978-1-7374675-4-0

Library of Congress Control Number: 2021912476

First edition July 2021

Cover design, layout, and publishing by Lauren Bartleson
Beaverton, OR

Cover photo by Nic Y-C on Unsplash

Published in the United States

Trigger warning

This book discusses mental health and mental illness, including anxiety, depression, suicide, eating disorders, and body dysmorphia.

Please take care while reading.

Disclaimer

The stories shared within are my personal experiences and are in no way a substitute for professional advice or support. Please seek the advice of a mental health professional or another qualified health provider to discuss your unique circumstances.

If you or someone you know is experiencing suicidal thoughts, call the Suicide Prevention Lifeline at 800-273-8255 or text HOME to the Crisis Text Line at 741741. These services are free and confidential. If you are located outside the United States, call your local emergency line.

To my mom, for everything.

It's a treadmill.
We can slow it down.
We can get off.

-Mom

Preface

Wednesday, May 12, 2021. 6:02 a.m.

My mom is no stranger to my insomnia. She's also intimately familiar with the constant state of burnout I always seem to be in.

For years, she's been not-so-subtly telling me to slow down. To take on less. To let something go.

Despite her best efforts, I've never listened. To her, I say, "I'll try; I've got it; don't worry," but inside, I'm telling myself, "I've got this; I can do it all. It's just one more thing."

This morning is no exception.

I just sent her a list of 50 haiku I wrote over the course of the last four hours with a witty introduction, joking that I wrote a book.

After responding with a quick, "Is this what you did all night? Omg!!" she sent a follow-up message with a note that stopped me in my tracks:

Lauren, having it all can be too much. In reading these all together, it paints a picture. It's kind of sad, with spurts of other emotions.

What if you try to reimagine a life without it ALL.

Maybe a cottage. Not a big home. Less financial chasing. Hobbies only for fun. Maybe even not chasing the promotion.

She ends with another nugget: *It's a treadmill.*

We can slow it down. We can get off.

Holy shit.

She's right.

I put myself in this situation: I climbed onto the treadmill. I turned the speed up, skipping right over the warm-up and going all the way to max, right from the get-go. Not only that, I've been increasing the incline at an unbearable rate.

I've never stopped, much less slowed down.

But I can.

I can slow down.

I can put my feet on the side and take a breather.

I can get off.

It's too much to bear
Sometimes, I feel like I can't
Usually I can

Introduction

I've been told I'm the epitome of a Virgo: reliable, sensible, practical, thoughtful. A perfectionist who is driven and hard-working in everything, but especially when it comes to my career. A creative who uses writing and art as an outlet. Someone who is extremely loyal, kind, and dedicated.

I've also been told I embody the negative traits of a Virgo: having such high standards that end up making me judgmental and critical towards others or being a chronic over-thinker who often comes off as stubborn or uptight when I'm confident about something.

This is me. To. A. Tee.

The thing is, I don't believe in astrology — or at least I thought I didn't.

The idea that stars and planets could influence our behavior and actions so heavily has never made sense to me.

Honestly, I struggle to understand what people mean when they say Mercury is in retrograde, and even after googling extensively, I don't really understand what rising sign, ruling planet, and ascendant mean. It's hard for me to grasp how the phases of the moon guide our life.

With all that said, I recently read about a phenomenon called "Saturn return," which very well might change my stance on astrology altogether.

In the literal sense, "Saturn return" is when Saturn returns to the place where it was when you were born.

Many astrologers believe that these "returns" define the stages and changes of life around ages 30, 60, and 90, based on the knowledge that it takes 29.5 years for Saturn to return home.

As I write this, it's 11 weeks after my 29.5-year mark — and I feel "Saturn return" in full force, like I'm drowning in a sea of existential questions and searching for answers that may never come.

Over the last year or so, I've been going through a very intense personal transformation period, likely in part because of the pandemic's forced isolation, but also, perhaps, because I'm going through my first "Saturn return." Who knows.

For as long as I can remember, I've felt this immense pressure to do it all, but nothing compares to how it's felt over the last few months.

On top of giving my normal 200% to everything and everyone, we bought a house, I took on an expanded role at work, and I started approximately a hundred new projects and hobbies (you're reading one!).

Add in extreme insomnia, anxiety, depression, and burnout, not to mention living through a global pandemic, a mental health crisis, and a loneliness epidemic, and it all became too much.

I hit my limit.

The breaking point, unfortunately (or fortunately) happened on a call with a colleague.

Before this conversation, I had talked to peers and colleagues about burnout in the kind-of-joking, kind-of-not way where we talk about meeting overload and feeling overwhelmed with a never-ending priority and to-do list, but never extreme burnout; the kind where you quite literally break down in tears because you're so overwhelmed by the idea of sending or receiving just one more email.

Yep, I did that.

That night, I was so desperate that I wrote a haiku begging for sleep. When I awoke a few hours later, I had this urge to keep writing. I asked myself what I was feeling and turned it into a second haiku.

Two poems became three, which became five, and suddenly I had a collection of 50 haiku documenting how I was feeling throughout my breaking point.

That's what this book is: the 50 haiku that I wrote in those early, predawn hours leading up to one of my darkest moments.

You'll read the poems in the exact order that I wrote them, giving you a glimpse into how I was thinking and feeling in each moment.

Before diving in, I want to acknowledge how fortunate I am to have access to healthcare, doctors, specialists, and medication. I'm also extremely grateful to have a strong support system of family and friends that care deeply about my personal well-being.

lauren bartleson

I am acutely aware that not everyone has these resources available to them, but if you are going through something similar, I hope you know there are resources and people there to support you.

As a friendly reminder: it's not a weakness to ask for help; on the contrary, it's a form of strength and bravery. By reaching out for support, you're saying "I'm worth fighting for."

In the weeks and months leading up to this moment, I felt truly and utterly alone. I knew I had loved ones that I could have reached out to, but I didn't want to bother anyone or feel like I was being a burden—and honestly, I felt like no one would really understand what I was going through.

It wasn't until I saw a thread of comments on a YouTube video following the tragic death of a van life influencer that I realized I wasn't alone.

Quite the opposite, in fact: there were dozens of comments from others who were navigating anxiety, depression, and burnout, just like I was.

Maybe it's just me, but I feel like there's this stigma around mental health, at least in the communities that I'm part of, both in-person and online; that admitting that you're not okay makes you look weak, less than.

Seeing all of those people saying, "You know what? I'm not okay and I'm getting help," made me realize there must be so many others out there who are struggling with the same challenges I am but who aren't comfortable talking about it.

I know with the utmost certainty that this won't be the last time I or others will experience these feelings, which is where this book comes in.

I wrote this book as a way to process what I went through, but I'm publishing it so I can have a physical reminder that I made it through the darkness once and can again. It's also a way of showing myself that I'm strong, creative, and driven enough to follow my own instincts and push myself out of my comfort zone.

As of publishing, I am in a healthier mental space. Even so, I hope these poems transport you back to the midnight hours of May 12, 2021, when I was in an entirely different place, experiencing seemingly every possible emotion in a matter of hours.

I admire those who are working to break the stigma around mental health and want to do my part. I hope my story helps those who are stuck in a dark place, like I was, realize they're not alone.

What is haibun?

As a long-form writer, it didn't feel right to share these haiku without context; there's so much more behind the seventeen syllables that needs to be said.

With that in mind, I started digging to see if there was a form of writing that paired haiku with other styles of writing to form a bigger story. Before long, I was introduced to — and completely enamored with — the world of haibun, a Japanese style of poetry created in the late 1600s that combines haiku and prose.

I learned that, while haiku tends to focus on nature, haibun typically focuses more on everyday experiences and discusses everything from food and family to moments, memories, and feelings.

It was exactly what I was looking for.

lauren bartleson

I read a haibun detailing how three generations of women gathered over enchiladas, margaritas, and ice cream, followed by another heart-wrenching tale of a late-night call from a woman's granddaughter telling her of the loss of their family cat.

I had an immediate sense that this writing style was completely and unequivocally me: it would allow me to share my story through haiku and prose and would be a challenge in all senses of the word.

While I grew up counting syllables and writing haiku for fun, I never thought of myself as a poet of any kind. In fact, it's only been in the last few years that I've started gravitating toward poetry as a reader.

This collection is very near and dear to my heart, and I'm excited to have it documented—for myself and others. Thank you for reading.

lauren bartleson

the beginning
(of the end)

lauren bartleson

Legs shaking, mind racing. Sleep little, rise when the clock strikes three. Six weeks and counting with no end in sight. It's time: I'm asking for help — from the body, the mind, the doctor. Hello? Anyone? Can you hear me?

lauren bartleson

the middle
(of the night)

lauren bartleson

anxious

Tears splash. Hiccups arise. Silent cries. I curl up as small as possible, trying to hide yet can't escape. The blue light: it follows, finding me wherever I go.

There's so much pressure
I am tired; it's all too much
When is it enough?

lauren bartleson

enchanted

Exploring continents, traveling light. It's an
experience; soak it all up: the sights, the souvenirs,
the smiling guides. When home calls, come back
only for so long.

They say don't settle
Sometimes I find it's enough
So why should I not?

lauren bartleson

agony

Panic. Prayer. PPE. These words, they fill our
heads, our minds, our eyes. For days, weeks,
months, with no end in sight. We repeat: it can't be
true. Denial, depression, devoid — they come in
waves, lingering too long.

We are not the same
COVID changed everything, yes?
Or is it just me?

24   lauren bartleson

infatuation

Words: they're in me. They become me. To others, a letter is just that: a thing on a page, a never-ending string broken by spaces. Yet to both, the story eventually comes; the message is revealed.

Crack myself open
I crave being raw, real
It makes me feel heard

lauren bartleson

depressed

Eyes heavy, mind tired, heart empty. We're there,
but only physically. We respond quickly, not
meeting their eye. Say okay, talk about the sky;
move on. Heads down, keep going. The cycle
never stops.

It's not what it seems
I say I'm fine but I'm not;
I am lost inside

lauren bartleson

powerless

Here, there; take, have. All day, we give and give
until there's nothing left. Time, love, energy — it
escapes us; come dusk, we're empty.

It is not selfish
To rest, to slow down, to breathe;
To fill your own cup

lauren bartleson

inadequate

Under photos, they say do this, not that. They tell
you how to live, what to wear, what to buy. They
let us inside, leading us to believe we're not good
enough; that we can't compare.

It is dangerous:
Self-diagnosis online;
Stop this game we play

lauren bartleson

blissful

Sit tall, heart over hips. Lean back, lie down; get
comfortable. Deep breaths: sharp inhale, slow
exhale. Again, again, again. Time ticks slowly,
breaths becoming bigger, longer — until the mind
clears (never).

A sense of calm comes
Washes over me; here, now
Even off the mat

lauren bartleson

overcome

Eyes closed, breath slow. My mat is beneath me but my mind is elsewhere, transported. You and me. Me and you. Bare feet, hardwood floors. It's dark, yet our black shadows glow from the fridge light. Arms twisted, hair intertwined; squeezing each other tight.

It is not a place
This moment, I imagined;
It is here, with you

lauren bartleson

inferior

Regret: it pulses through me. Aching, never letting go. I try to move on but it fails, time and time again. The memories fade yet they always stay.

Forgiving myself:
It is so hard to let go,
But I need to heal

lauren bartleson

agitated

We're running, our feet sprinting, trying to keep up. The pings, the rings, the beeps — it's all too much. Calendars crammed, feeling tired and useless. Day after day, we struggle. Together, we're just trying to survive.

I say it often:
I'm too busy; too stressed out
Then why keep pushing?

lauren bartleson

sorrow

The feelings come flooding back: the good times, the bad, the scary; the wishing, the wanting, the regretting. It's been years, but sometimes it feels like you're still here.

What I wish I said:
It wasn't you; it was all me
I did this to us

42   lauren bartleson

dismayed

Exhaustion hits. Stress, anxiety, depression: they blur together, one becoming the other; becoming me. Yes, yes, yes. It's always yes, even when I mean no.

Being an empath:
I need to set boundaries
It's hard — way too hard

lauren bartleson

resentful

Scrolling, scrolling, scrolling. Green juice. Scroll.
Second workout of the day; no, wait: third. Swipe.
Paleo, keto, plant-based — try them all. Buy this
book, try this cleanse, follow this expert. Everyone
says, "be just like me." When is enough, enough?

It scares me, my past:
How I let myself get there
Orthorexia

lauren bartleson

grief

The news: it hits hard. The same photo, splashed
across the homepage of every website, the
clickbait titles luring me in. Her smiling face,
now just a memory. I'm instantly triggered,
seeing myself in her story. My heart is breaking,
shattering. I'm saying goodbye.

It's okay to grieve
One you've never met before
To curl up; wallow

lauren bartleson

relieved

The advice they give is simple: travel every
weekend, run every race, go to every party. West
Coast, East Coast: you name it, I do it; never
stopping, never breathing. Always planning.

I did not know it:
Becoming a homebody;
It's me, deep inside

lauren bartleson

euphoric

Black, barely visible; the vast unknown lies ahead.
There's nothing; wait, something: the lights in the
distance, they sparkle, draw my eye. I look away,
blink. Suddenly, the world is alive.

My favorite time
When darkness fades; sun rises
The colors: stunning

lauren bartleson

longing

Silence, stillness — it draws me in; sits there
taunting me, like it's close enough to touch yet far
enough away that I'll never be able to feel it or
experience its glory.

It is my mantra:
Embracing simplicity;
It's what gets me through

lauren bartleson

helpless

They say they're taboo, words like depression
and anxiety and burnout, but to me, they're
anything but. I feel them, I see them — every day,
every hour, every minute. They're part of me;
roommates that never leave.

Breaking the stigma:
It's scary, showing the world
This deep part of me

lauren bartleson

satisfied

The smell of freshly-ground beans, the sound of milk steaming and whirring, the perfect ratio of crema: together, it's perfection.

My morning routine:
It is sacred; just for me
The quiet brings calm

lauren bartleson

content

Stillness: it's something I crave but can seemingly never achieve. I'm always doing something — anything — to distract myself from myself, my thoughts.

Slowing down my mind:
It is more important now
Than ever before

lauren bartleson

stimulated

My mind, I can't turn it off; thoughts run in
circles, never stopping, barely slowing — every
day, another marathon finished.

Before bed, it's key:
Yoga and meditation,
Followed by reading

lauren bartleson

guilty

Deadlines, decisions, deliverables: they're there at all times; day, night, and every moment in between. I can never escape.

Work is not just work;
It is also when thinking
Away from it all

lauren bartleson

fondness

Letters scrambled; one word, two, three, then four
— slowly but surely, we figure them out, finding
our way to the chuckle that inevitably comes.

Sundays growing up;
My favorite memory:
Jumbles at breakfast

lauren bartleson

sentimental

Sometimes, I miss it: the misty mornings, the
Cypress trees looming over the cliffs, the sun
rising slowly, the sand in my shoes. And then I
remember — it will always be home.

Took it for granted:
The salt air, the ocean waves
Walks along the beach

lauren bartleson

rapture

The coffee shops, the bridges, the bookstore;
for what feels like the first time, I take a deep
breath, soaking in the fresh air, lush greenery, and
mountain views. I am here, now.

Portland, Oregon:
Every day, I'm so grateful
To call this place home

lauren bartleson

triumphant

Letting go: what does that even mean? Because,
I remind myself, change is good. It's a new
beginning: for me, for mental freedom.

This switch: it feels like
Giving myself permission
To own who I am

lauren bartleson

perplexed

The deep conversations we refer to: the weather,
food, work — but what about living in darkness,
trying to overcome yourself? Are those true, too?
Apparently not.

They say it's taboo
To talk about mental health
Why? I don't get it

74   lauren bartleson

exasperated

Constantly comparing, changing who we are to be bigger, better, brighter; trying to take up more space, more energy, more light. Will we ever be enough?

Wanting more, more, more
"I should be happy," I say
Yet it's not enough

lauren bartleson

insecure

Could, should, right, wrong: these words haunt
me, making me question every move, every
word, every action. The cycle never breaks; it just
expands.

Am I not enough?
I ask myself constantly;
Keep wondering why

78   lauren bartleson

disillusioned

I struggle to stay afloat, these thoughts — the
expectations — are plaguing my mind and
dragging me deeper and deeper into the abyss.
Will it always be this way?

I live out my life
Based on what others believe
Or so I assume

lauren bartleson

hopeful

I try to convince myself it's not a lie — that if I
were to leave, someone, anyone, would care, but
the question keeps coming: how do I feel so alone
when I'm surrounded by so many, so much?

Friendship is a gift
A reason; season; lifetime
It doesn't matter which

lauren bartleson

aggravated

I hold on tightly: not to the love or the affection
or the validation — but to the negative; the one in
ten. As they say, misery breeds company.

Community? No
Instagram; YouTube; online;
The trolls are toxic

lauren bartleson

jovial

The everyday love: it's something kind of special;
the little moments that no one but us will see,
knowing those will be the ones that I will come
back to again and again, forever.

Our daily routine:
Minis, dinner, Jeopardy
I love it so much

lauren bartleson

frustrated

The couch, the cushions, the comfort: it pulls me in, deep into the dark unknown, teasing me with its uncertainty and lifelessness.

My eyes are heavy
I feel drained beyond belief
Why can't I sleep now?

lauren bartleson

satisfied

Ten years; the same routine day in and day out,
keeping me grounded and alive; giving me
something to look forward to: the sweet smell of
early mornings.

I can't get enough:
The first sip of a latte,
The warmth brings me joy

lauren bartleson

annoyed

Like depression, it's part of me. It's in me, it's who
I am. Work to live feels unattainable, a longing
that I wish for but will never have.

A workaholic:
It's a thing; it's who I am
I can't let it go

lauren bartleson

passion

Uncertainty comes out in every word; every
comma feels out of place, every synonym
insurmountable — together it feels forced,
inauthentic, unsteady.

Writing a full book:
I've dreamt about it for years
Am I ready yet?

lauren bartleson

affectionate

There are no words — only love, respect,
admiration, aspiration. To you, from me:

Dad, you are the best
I love you more than you know
How long for? Always

lauren bartleson

romantic

Thinking back to the day we met — the time, the date, the place, the people; at that moment, I knew: it was you all along.

On a coffee date:
Chai tea, conversation, you
It's my favorite

lauren bartleson

touched

When I'm feeling lost and alone, stuck inside my mind, it's not a person that drags me out, it's a place, a feeling, a love so deep: it's home.

Oregon, my love
Thank you for bringing me back
To myself, truly

lauren bartleson

eager

Trying, again and again; attempting to fit in, to feel
wanted. It's not until I do it for me — in a place
and way that no one sees — that it falls into place.

Am I a yogi?
I practice at night, daily;
Does that count? Sort of?

102   lauren bartleson

dread

It lures me in, like a drink that I'll never have, a cigarette I'll never smoke, a drug I'll never take; even so, it's there, always pulling me back, never letting go.

Social media:
It's no longer obsession
Now it's addiction

lauren bartleson

hurt

It's exhausting putting yourself out there; it's
draining and daunting and demeaning, telling me
I'm not worth it, worth you — but I am; I will be.
One day.

I felt stuck; alone
I needed your help, support
To take the first step

lauren bartleson

disappointed

Three little numbers that add up to so much; they
guide my life: what I eat, what I wear, how I
feel. Will they steal my life, my time, my sanity
forever?

The numbers, the weight
It caused a downward spiral
Yet I still hold on

lauren bartleson

nervous

The memories: they flood back as I try to fill the gaps of my childhood, realizing that, although I felt alone, I never really was; I had a community, a language, a culture that would be there to return to when I need it the most.

Maybe, just maybe
I'm starting to find my way
Back home, to my faith

lauren bartleson

proud

18 years of suffering — under the weight of
someone else's words, expectations; trauma: it
becomes me, it defines me, it is me.

Your words, they hurt me;
You made me miserable
I'm stronger for it

lauren bartleson

compassionate

For the first time, I see it: what life could look like if I were to live fearlessly—for me and only me. Frankly, it scares me. What if I'm not good enough? Oh, but what if I am?

I often forget
To thank my body, my mind
For making me, me

114   lauren bartleson

the end
(of the beginning)

lauren bartleson

Just five more minutes
Actually, I can't do it
I'll sleep forever

118   lauren bartleson

Author's note

As I said in the introduction, I felt very alone in the days and weeks leading up to this experience.

Maybe it's just me, but I feel like there's this expectation to always be "okay," even if you're not.

When I'm in a dark place, I find it's easier to put on a smile and make it seem like everything's okay rather than trying to explain how deeply I'm struggling, especially since others can't physically see things like anxiety, depression, and chronic illness.

What no one knows is that moment — the moment that I convinced myself to wake up and get out of bed — took every ounce of energy I had. Opening my eyes was a challenge I didn't know I could do. Each step to get downstairs, to a place where I could hug my husband, felt like I was dragging a stack of bricks behind me.

If you're in the midst of a difficult season, I hope this book can be the friend to you that I wished I had during this time.

In addition, I hope my story reminds you that it's okay not to be okay. When I'm struggling, I try to remind myself: breathe; this too shall pass.

I also hope this book inspires you to talk more openly about topics like anxiety, depression, burnout, and suicidal ideation with those you trust, whether it's with a partner, parent, sibling, friend, doctor, licensed professional, or someone on the other end of an anonymous hotline.

Believe me when I say that I understand that talking about these things is incredibly difficult, especially the first time you say it out loud.

lauren bartleson

When I got the courage to tell my husband about
the dark thoughts that came and stayed, I couldn't
breathe through the tears.

When I tried to tell my mom what happened,
I couldn't pick up the phone. I was convinced
that no words would come out of my mouth, so
instead, I wrote a text message, hands shaking as I
put the experience into writing for the first time.

It took minutes of hovering over the little blue
circle before I was able to press the icon that
would make my message instantly appear on her
phone 700 miles away.

When I called my brother five days later, my hand
was shaking uncontrollably as I held my phone
and recounted what I had been through.

It would be over a week before I had the courage
to bring it up in a conversation with my dad.

I say all of this to acknowledge the strength it takes to share your experience out loud. It's scary and terrifying and emotional and exhausting and overwhelming and a lot just to say "I'm not okay," much less put the weight of dark and negative feelings into words.

Quite frankly, I'm scared —
To fail, to be judged, to fall
Alone, together

Please remember that you are not alone.

I am here with you. I see you. I feel you.

With love,

Lauren

Acknowledgments

Mom — I don't know where to start. I suppose with "thank you," but those two small words don't even start to convey how grateful I am for you and your support. Since day one, you have been my biggest cheerleader. In fact, when I was reimagining the direction of the book, you were the first person I shared my ideas with (don't tell Matt!). You were, and will always be, my first beta reader, editor, and brainstorm partner. In a way, you're even my personal publicist, sharing my work with your network. I think you're also unknowingly part life coach and therapist on top of being a lawyer. Your most important role, though, is my mom. I truly couldn't envision any better mother in the world. I know these words aren't enough, but thank you for everything. I love you.

Dad — I learned the importance of discipline and dedication from you, and while I admittedly struggle with them sometimes, they're traits that I'm immensely grateful to have. It's because of you that I'm so driven, inspired, passionate, and invested in my work. I'm not just saying this, but you are truly the most inspiring person I know. I admire you so much and will always, always look up to you. It's an honor to be your daughter.

Every night, you ask:
"Who loves you?" and "How long for?"
I say, "You," "Always"

Karen — Thank you for being one of the first to read *Insomnia*. Because of your editing magic, this book is even better than I could have imagined. Thank you for your love and endless support.

Justin — I will never forget how you showed up for me during this time. Hearing you say, "I have space for you. If you're feeling too much, give it to me. I can hold it for you," is a feeling that I will honestly cherish forever. You are so much more than a brother to me; you're a friend, a leader, a teacher, a guide. I love you.

Put it all on me
I promise you're not alone
Remember, I'm here

Janette — You came into my life for a reason, a season, AND a lifetime, and I will forever be grateful to call you a friend. I truly don't know what I would do without you. Thank you for everything. I appreciate you so much, twinnie.

Matt — I am grateful beyond belief to not only know you, but to call you my husband, my best friend, my love, my family. I know I put you through a lot and that this was a scary, emotional, and overwhelming time for you. I'm genuinely sorry for causing any pain and sadness. I don't even know how to explain how much I appreciate your love, concern, and support, and I promise to do everything in my power to try to make you happy and proud from here on out. I love you so, so much. Thank you for everything.

Georgia — thank you: for the love, the cuddles, the snuggles, the kisses, the walks; for loving me unconditionally. When you're next to me, I never feel alone.

lauren bartleson

Lauren Bartleson is a digital storyteller and communications manager who lives near Portland, Oregon, with her husband, Matt, and their dog, Georgia. By sharing the raw, open, and vulnerable stories that are helping her heal, she hopes to do her part to help break the stigma around mental health.

This is her debut book and foray into poetry.

Made in the USA
Columbia, SC
22 July 2021